The
OBAMA
FAMILY
Photo Album

Celebrating
FIRST LADY
MICHELLE OBAMA
in Pictures

Jane Katirgis

Enslow Publishers, Inc.
40 Industrial Road
Box 398
Berkeley Heights, NJ 07922
USA
http://www.enslow.com

For Dorothy, Nicole, Ali, Pam, and Lindsey —
Thank you, ladies, for all your help with this book!

Library of Congress Cataloging-in-Publication Data:
Katirgis, Jane.
 Celebrating first lady Michelle Obama in pictures / Jane Katirgis.
    p. cm. — (The Obama family photo album)
 Includes bibliographical references and index.
 Summary: "Photographs illustrate the life of Michelle Obama from childhood with a focus on her role as first lady of the United States"—Provided by publisher.
 ISBN-13: 978-0-7660-3652-9
 ISBN-10: 0-7660-3652-9
 1. Obama, Michelle, 1964– —Pictorial works—Juvenile literature. 2. Presidents' spouses—United States—Biography—Pictorial works—Juvenile literature. I. Title.
 E909.K37 2009
 973.932092—dc22
 [B]
                    2009009288

Printed in the United States of America

10 9 8 7 6 5 4 3 2 1

To Our Readers:
We have done our best to make sure all Internet Addresses in this book were active and appropriate when we went to press. However, the author and the publisher have no control over and assume no liability for the material available on those Internet sites or on other Web sites they may link to. Any comments or suggestions can be sent by e-mail to comments@enslow.com or to the address on the back cover.

♻ Enslow Publishers, Inc., is committed to printing our books on recycled paper. The paper in every book contains 10% to 30% post-consumer waste (PCW). The cover board on the outside of each book contains 100% PCW. Our goal is to do our part to help young people and the environment too!

Photo Credits: Associated Press, pp. 1, 3, 11, 13, 15, 16, 19, 20, 21, 23, 29 (bottom); Barack Obama Campaign p. 6; Corey Lowenstein/MCT/Landov, p. 17; Daniel Gluskoter/UPI/Landov, p. 14; © David Burnett/Contact Press Images, p. 12; Jason Reed/Reuters/Landov, pp. 18, 22; Jonathan Ernst/Reuters/Landov, p. 27; Joshua Roberts/
Reuters/Landov, p. 26; Joyce N. Boghosian/MAI/Landov, p. 28; Kevin Dietsch/UPI/Landov, pp. 5, 31; Kevin Lamarque/Reuters/Landov, pp. 29 (top), 30; Larry Downing/Reuters/Landov, pp. 24–25; Olivier Douliery/MCT/Landov, p. 10; Polaris Images, pp. 7, 8; University of Chicago, p. 9.

Cover Photo: Jim Young/Reuters/Landov

Contents

A Modern Woman

She is a graduate of Princeton University and Harvard Law School. She has trained a new generation of community leaders. She is the mother of two children, and she is first lady of the United States of America. She is Michelle Obama.

At five feet, eleven inches tall, Michelle Obama gets noticed. But it is her historic entry into the White House, as the first African-American first lady, that has captured the world's attention. The great-great granddaughter of a slave, Michelle has become an important figure in American history. It all started with a simple and hard-working family in Chicago.

Growing Up

Michelle LaVaughn Robinson was born on January 17, 1964, in Chicago, Illinois. She grew up with her parents, Fraser and Marian Robinson, and her brother, Craig. Michelle's father had a disease called multiple sclerosis, but he hardly ever missed a day of work. Michelle says, "He was our champion, our hero. . . . He never stopped smiling and laughing, even while struggling to button his shirt, even while using two canes to get himself across the room to give my mom a kiss. He just woke up a little earlier and he worked a little harder."

This photo was taken when Michelle was in elementary school in Chicago. Both Michelle and her brother skipped second grade.

College and Career

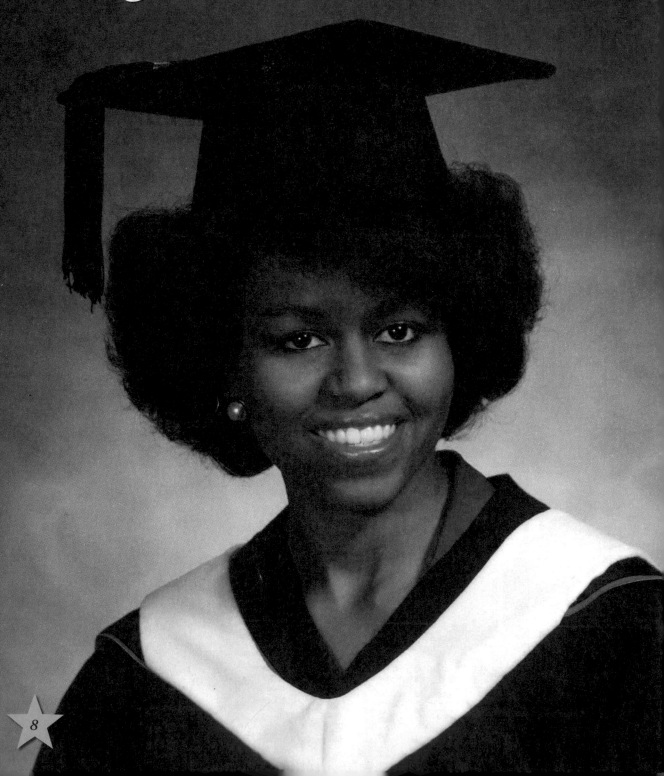

Michelle graduated from Princeton University in 1985. She studied sociology and African-American studies. Michelle says that she and her brother were both able to go to college thanks to her parents' hard work.

In 1988, Michelle graduated from Harvard Law School. At first, she worked as a lawyer. After three years, she left the law firm to take jobs helping her community. One of the jobs was to help college students find ways to volunteer in the community near their school. She is shown here when she was Associate Dean of Student Services & Director of the University Community Service Center at the University of Chicago.

Becoming a Wife and Mom

*B*arack and Michelle were married on October 18, 1992. Malia was born in 1998, and Sasha was born in 2001.

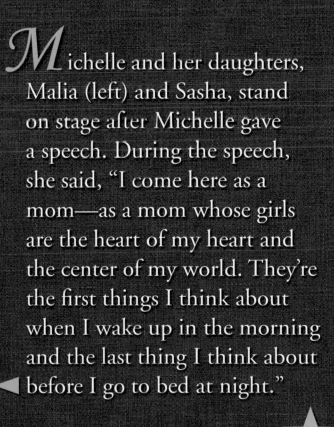

*M*ichelle and her daughters, Malia (left) and Sasha, stand on stage after Michelle gave a speech. During the speech, she said, "I come here as a mom—as a mom whose girls are the heart of my heart and the center of my world. They're the first things I think about when I wake up in the morning and the last thing I think about before I go to bed at night."

Fitness and Fun

$\mathcal{M}$ichelle enjoys some hula-hoop time with Sasha at a Fourth of July picnic in Montana. She also likes barbecues and french fries!

$\mathcal{M}$ichelle likes to be active. "Exercise is really important to me. . . . If I'm ever feeling tense or stressed or like I'm about to have a meltdown, I'll put on my iPod and head to the gym or out on a bike ride along Lake Michigan with the girls."

While her husband was running for president, Michelle Obama joined him at some events during his campaign across the country. Here she speaks at a rally on a college campus in Las Vegas, Nevada.

Michelle takes a photo with a supporter at a rally in Ohio.

A crowd welcomes Michelle Obama to the Democratic National Convention in August 2008, where she makes a speech.

*M*ichelle writes her own speeches and does not read from notes.

Election Day

*A*fter a two-year campaign, Barack Obama won the presidential election on Tuesday, November 4, 2008. The Obama family waves to the crowd during the election night victory rally in Chicago.

*M*ichelle and Barack Obama cast their votes at a polling place in Chicago on election day.

Introduction to the White House

*F*irst Lady Laura Bush and Michelle Obama sit in a private room of the White House on Monday, November 10, 2008. Barack had won the election the previous week.

*P*resident George W. Bush and First Lady Laura Bush welcome President-elect Obama and Michelle Obama to the White House in Washington, D.C.

Inauguration Day

Michelle Obama holds the Bible that Abraham Lincoln used at his inauguration in 1861 as her husband takes the presidential oath of office. Inauguration day, January 20, 2009, was attended by more than one million people at the nation's capital, and it was celebrated throughout the world.

President Barack Obama and First Lady Michelle Obama get ready to dance at one of the ten inaugural balls they attended on inauguration night, January 20, 2009.

First Lady

On her first day as first lady, Michelle Obama shakes hands with members of the public. They have come to tour the White House.

Community Life in D.C.

*F*irst Lady Michelle Obama reads to children at Mary's Center, a community health center in Washington, D.C.

*M*ichelle Obama hugs a school girl after a performance for children at the White House in February 2009.

27

Healthy Food Starts at Home

On the first day of spring in 2009, local students help the first lady dig a space for an organic vegetable garden at the White House.

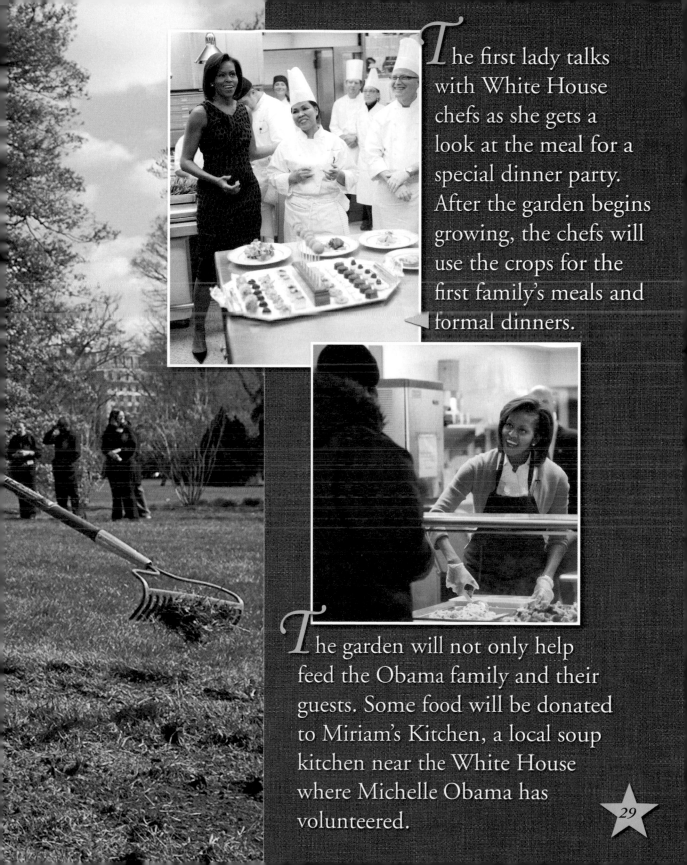

The first lady talks with White House chefs as she gets a look at the meal for a special dinner party. After the garden begins growing, the chefs will use the crops for the first family's meals and formal dinners.

The garden will not only help feed the Obama family and their guests. Some food will be donated to Miriam's Kitchen, a local soup kitchen near the White House where Michelle Obama has volunteered.

29

Mom-in-Chief

*M*ichelle Obama leads her family, including daughters Sasha (left) and Malia. Her mother, Marian Robinson, joins President Obama behind them. They walk from the Marine One helicopter after spending a weekend at their home in Chicago. Michelle is a busy mother, wife, and first lady of the United States of America.

*T*he family enjoys walking their dog, Bo, on the South Lawn of the White House.

Further Reading

Books

Bausum, Ann. *Our Country's First Ladies.* Washington, D.C.: National Geographic, 2007.

Brophy, David Bergen. *Michelle Obama: Meet the First Lady.* New York: HarperCollins, 2008.

The National Children's Book and Literacy Alliance. *Our White House: Looking In, Looking Out.* Somerville, Mass.: Candlewick Press, 2008.

Internet Addresses

Kids.gov. *The Official Kids' Portal for the U.S. Government.* http://www.kids.gov

The White House. *First Lady Michelle Obama.* http://www.whitehouse.gov/administration/michelle_obama/

Index